EQUIPPED FOR LIFE

EPHESIANS, PHILIPPIANS, COLOSSIANS

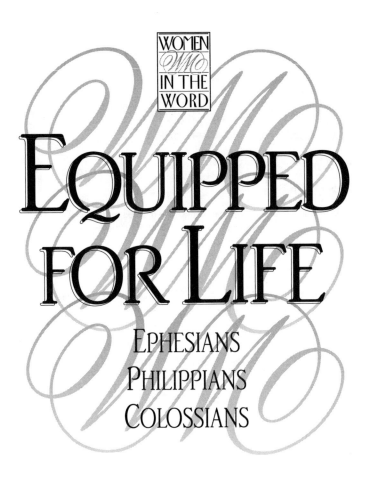

WOMEN
WHO
IN THE
WORD

EQUIPPED
FOR LIFE

EPHESIANS
PHILIPPIANS
COLOSSIANS

Linda McGinn

Baker Books

A Division of Baker Book House Co
Grand Rapids, Michigan 49516

© 1994 by Linda McGinn

Published by Baker Books,
a division of Baker Book House Company
P.O. Box 6287 Grand Rapids, Michigan 49516-6287

Printed in the United States of America

ISBN 0-8010-3876-6

CONTENTS

INTRODUCTION

We live in a critical time. Within our secular society opposition to Christianity mounts daily. It is imperative that we prepare to stand firm in our faith in the days to come.

Corrie ten Boom, Dutch survivor of the Nazi World War II concentration camps, spoke at a banquet my husband and I attended in 1977. Using Paul's words she described God's challenge to her as she faced inconceivable persecution from the Nazis. "Finally, be strong in the Lord," writes Paul, "and in his mighty power. Put on the full armor of God so that you can take your stand against the devil's schemes . . . Therefore put on the full armor of God, so that when the day of evil comes, you may be able to stand your ground, and after you have done everything, to stand. Stand firm then." (Ephesians 6:10–14a)

Her Dutch accent and broken English only accentuated her fervent plea, "When the enemy came in like a flood, I ran into Jesus' arms and reminded myself of Paul's words. Stand, stand, and stand again! I say stand up!"

In response to cultural antagonism toward the gospel and echoing Corrie ten Boom's words, I have titled this study, *Equipped for Life* with the intent of helping every Christian prepare for a life of strength and courage in the Lord Jesus Christ. The study is in three sections: *Ephesians*: Equipped to Stand, *Philippians*: Equipped to Walk, and *Colossians*: Equipped to Trust.

I pray this study will enable you to draw intimately near to the Lord Jesus and equip you to stand in this evil day.

As group leaders prepare their lessons, they are encouraged to use the accompanying leader's guide which contains commentary and lesson summaries.

A COUNTRY
NOT UNLIKE OUR OWN

Paul, apostle and servant of Jesus Christ by the will of God, finds himself in a Roman prison awaiting a hearing from the present caesar of the day, Nero. Paul writes letters to four church bodies located in Ephesus, Philippi, Colosse. Messengers take Paul's letters to their own home towns. Tychicus from Ephesus, Epaphroditus from Philippi, Epaphras from Colosse, and Philemon, a runaway slave whose master also lived in Colosse. In this study, *Equipped for Life*, we will be exploring the text of the first three letters.

Paul's intent in writing these letters was to encourage and thank the believers for their interest in him and support of his ministry. The focus of his letters is to offer further insight and explanation about God's intent for his Church, the body of his Son Jesus Christ. Included are profound descriptions of the person and work of Jesus Christ, as well as directives for personal Christian living and harmonious community living among the brothers and sisters in Christ. Paul also warns against the false teachers who distort the truth and admonishes believers to hold firmly to the pure gospel of Jesus Christ.

Ephesus, Philippi, and Colosse were located in what is now the country of Turkey. The economy was prosperous in each and a mix of nationalities was present. Oriental and Greek culture dominated Ephesus. A Roman and Greek cultural mix characterized the others. Paul designed his letters to reach a predominantly Gentile constituency. This reflected Paul's call from God to preach the gospel to the Gentiles.

Written sometime around A.D. 62–64, Paul's prison epistles to these churches in Asia Minor are a rich source of instruction and explanation for us today as we seek to live the Christian life in a way that brings glory to the Lord Jesus Christ. We discover new aspects of Christ's character. We learn of the spiritual battle that rages around us and the Spirit's power to prevail through us. We come to understand anew the depths of God's love for us. Christ's mission to reconcile us to God through his life, death, and resurrection is never more poignantly portrayed. May we read Paul's words not as literature, but as the very Word of God to us useful for "teaching, rebuking, correcting and training in righteousness" (2 Timothy 3:16).

EPHESIANS 1

God in the flesh walked among us. Why did he do this? Who is Jesus?

Paul answers these and more questions as he retells the remarkable facts of Christ's work on earth. Marveling, Paul goes on to explain the immediate benefits given all those who believe in God's Son, Jesus. Join Paul as he reflects with wonder on Christ's life, death, resurrection, and mission.

How does Christ's life affect you?

DAY 1

1. **Read Ephesians 1:1–2.**

   From these verses, list five facts you learn about this letter.

2.   Define *apostle* and *saint* in your own words.

3.   (a) Do you consider yourself a "saint"? Why or why not?

     (b) What do you believe are the identifying character qualities of a "saint" and how do these apply to your life?

─────────────────────────────────────── DAY 2

4.   **Read Ephesians 1:3–10**
        How does each phrase below reflect what God has accomplished?

v. 3 blessed us

v. 4 chose us

v. 5 predestined us

v. 7 have redemption

v. 9 made known to us

5.   According to verses 6 and 10, what are God's purposes
      for having done these things?

v. 6

v. 10

6.   Which aspect of God's work on your behalf are you most
      grateful for today? Why? Thank him now for this aspect
      of his love.

——————————————————————————————————————— DAY 3

7.   **Read Ephesians 1:11-14.**
      Paraphrase these verses in your own words.

8. (a) List aspects of your salvation described in verses 13–14.

    (b) What is the Holy Spirit's role in our lives as God's saved people?

9.   God has accomplished everything in Ephesians 1:3–14 "for the praise of His glory."

    (a) How would you define this phrase?

    (b) How can this phrase be fulfilled in and through your life today?

10. **Read Ephesians 1:15–19.**
    From these verses, what can we learn about prayer?

11. List the specific requests Paul makes for those he loves.

12. How specifically do you pray? Are your requests for others similar to Paul's? On a separate sheet of paper, copy the following headings. For the next month keep an accurate account of your prayers. Await God's response with faith and anticipation. Come in four weeks prepared to share with others in your small group the results of this month of prayer.

    Name

    Request

Scripture Verse

Date of Request
Answer

Date of Answer

=== DAY 5

13.   **Read Ephesians 1:19–23.**
        Paul's desire is that we know God's "incomparable great
        power for us who believe." List with verses the results
        of that great power made available to us by Christ.

14. How is Christ represented in our world today and how do we take part in this manifestation of Jesus Christ?

15. We live in a critical time in history. How does an understanding of God's power affect you today? Write a prayer here expressing these feelings and thoughts to God.

EPHESIANS 2

Separated from Christ, excluded from relationship with God—this is our life before belief in God's Son.

United with Christ, full access to and the privilege of relationship with the Father—this is our gift when we place our faith in Jesus Christ.

Once we were far away, but we are drawn near to God when we believe. Joined with all others who also believe, we become God's family in whom God's Spirit lives.

Learn more about God's family. How can you belong to God's family? How can you be his child?

=== DAY 1

1. **Read Ephesians 2:1–5.**

   Carefully list those phrases that describe our lives apart from Jesus Christ.

2.   What did God do to change our situation? Why?

3.   Reflect back on your life.

(a) Write phrases that describe your attitudes and actions when you were "dead in transgressions."

(b) If you have accepted Christ's offer of forgiveness, God's powerful intervention has raised you from death to new life in Christ. Thank God now for specific changes you see in your life as a result of his transforming power.

────────────────────────────────── Day 2

4.   **Read Ephesians 2:6–10.**

As described in this passage, what did God do for us in Christ Jesus?

5.   What was God's purpose as indicated in verse 7?

6. (a) In verses 8–10, what do you learn about your ability to
        accomplish God's purposes?

    (b) What does James 3:13–18 teach you about self-effort?

    (c) In which ways do you attempt to accomplish God's pur-
        poses in your own strength?

(d) Humbly turn from this sin and ask God for his empowering Holy Spirit to accomplish his purposes in your life.

7.   **Read Ephesians 2:11–12.**
      List key phrases that describe our situation without Christ.

8.   We were not only separated from God, but also from his chosen people who were to fulfill his plans and purposes in the world. Choose phrases from these verses which further explain this truth.
      Psalm 147:19

Romans 3:1–2

Romans 9:4–5

9.   Remember and describe your feelings of isolation and
        separation before coming to God through Christ.

    Now thank God for his abundant love that chose to bring
you to himself through Jesus Christ his Son.

─────────────────────────────────────── DAY 4

10.   **Read Ephesians 2:13–18.**
    (a) List the phrases in this passage that contain the word
        peace.

(b) Define *peace* in your own words.

11.   Write phrases that describe how this peace was accomplished.

12.   The Lord Jesus died and shed his blood that you might have peace.

(a) Are you experiencing God's peace today?

(b) From the following verses, list phrases related to peace. Ask God for his supernatural peace.
Psalm 119:165

Isaiah 26:3

Isaiah 32:17

John 14:27

John 16:33

━━━━━━━━━━━━━━━━━━━━━━━━━━━━━━ DAY 5

13.   **Read Ephesians 2:19–22.**
       Describe our new position in Christ.

14.   In twenty-five words or less write your definition of the body of Christ based on these verses.

15.   From these passages, what do you learn about Jesus Christ and about yourself as a member of his body? 1 Corinthians 3:9–11

        1 Corinthians 3:16–17

        1 Peter 2:4–10

16. (a) Write the verse from this week's study which holds the greatest meaning for you today and explain why you chose it.

(b) Describe one action you can take this week that reflects the impact of that verse on your life.

EPHESIANS 3

God's hidden mystery: through faith in Jesus Christ, Jews and Gentiles alike become children of God. They become members of one family and sharers in all the promises of God.

As those who believe in Jesus, we can approach God as Father with freedom and confidence. We also can know a love which surpasses human knowledge: Christ's love. Learn about this love which fills us with the fullness of God himself.

How can you experience this love beyond human measure?

DAY 1

1. **Read Ephesians 3:1–6.**

    How does Paul describe himself in this passage and what do you think he means by this description?

2. What is this "mystery" of which Paul speaks? Read Romans 11:1–27 for further insight.

3. (a) Which aspect of God's "mystery" is most significant to you today? Why?

   (b) How does this knowledge about God affect the way you live this week?

Day 2

4.   **Read Ephesians 3:7–9.**

   (a) Use Acts 9:1–20 to describe Paul's life prior to his experience with Jesus Christ.

Galatians 1:11–17

Philippians 3:4–9

1 Timothy 1:12–16

(b) How does this affect Paul's understanding of the "working of his power" (v. 7)?

5.   Explain the phrase in verse 8 "the unsearchable riches
of Christ" from your study of Ephesians to this point.
(If you know other verses which apply, list here.)

6.   How have you seen God's power working in your life?
        Come prepared to describe one incident to your group.

--- DAY 3

7.   **Read Ephesians 3:10–12.**
        Explain your understanding of verse 10.

8.   Use the following verses to describe what it means to
        approach God "with freedom and confidence."

        Hebrews 4:14–16

        Hebrews 10:19–23

1 John 2:28

1 John 4:16–18

9. (a) How is your relationship with God (and more specifi-
        cally your prayer life) affected by your understanding
        of this passage?

    (b) Write a prayer here thanking God for the "privilege" of
        his presence in prayer.

10.   **Read Ephesians 3:13–19.**
        List the different aspects of Paul's prayer.

11. (a) Which aspect of this prayer do you desire for yourself
        today?

    (b) Which aspect of this prayer do you desire for a specific
        family member or friend?

12. (a) Ask God by his grace, according to his will, to accomplish these things in your life and the life of your relative or friend.

    (b) Thank him for his active care and participation in your life even at this moment as you pray.

—————————————————————————————— Day 5

13.   **Read Ephesians 3:20–21.**
       What assurance do you receive from verse 20?

14.   What is God's ultimate purpose in every aspect of your life as seen in verse 21?

15.   Describe ways that God's glory can be seen through
        your life according to the following verses.
        Romans 4:20–21

        1 Corinthians 10:31–33

        2 Corinthians 3:18

16.   Name one way you can show God's glory today.

EPHESIANS 4

Relationships within God's family are very important to him. He wants his relatives to be humble, gentle, patient, and to bear with one another lovingly.

How can we do that? Each of us has been allocated his grace to make that behavior possible. Grace to care for one another and gifts to share with one another are God's equipment for our growth and strengthening.

God gives us the supernatural power to behave differently from those who do not know his Son. Learn about acceptable family behavior in God's household. How can you become a pleasing member of the family?

DAY 1

1. **Read Ephesians 4:1–6.**

    From the first three verses, list Paul's instructions to us as believers.

2. Define each of the following phrases:

One body

One Spirit

One hope

One Lord

One faith

One baptism

One God and Father

3. (a) What comfort do you receive from realizing that your God and Father is "over all, through all, and in all"?

   (b) How do you think that knowledge will affect the way you live?

━━━━━━━━━━━━━━━━━━━━━━━━━━━━━━━━━━━━━ DAY 2

4.   **Read Ephesians 4:7–13.**
   (a) Describe the gifts being given in each of the following passages.

Romans 12:3–8

2 Corinthians 12:7–11

Ephesians 4:7–13

(b) Who is the giver?

5.   Use verse 13 to identify the goal being accomplished.

6. (a) Which gifts do you believe God has given you?

(b) Are you using them that this goal might be accomplished?

(c) Ask God to use you and the gifts he has given you for his glory, honor, and praise.

─── Day 3

7.   **Read Ephesians 4:14–16.**

       List the benefits we receive when we ask God to use us for his glory, and exercise the gifts he has given us.

8.   Write a paragraph here which describes your understanding of Christ's body, the Church.

9.   What can you do today that will help you to grow in
      your relationship with Christ and his body, the Church?

━━━━━━━━━━━━━━━━━━━━━━━━━━━━━━━━━━━━ Day 4

10.   **Read Ephesians 4:17–24.**
      Contrast the attitudes and actions of non-Christians
      (those without Christ) with those who are Christians
      (noting verse numbers).

      Those without Christ   Those belonging to Christ
      v. 17   v. 19

      v. 18   v. 20

11.   Which quality in this passage describes you? Explain.

12.   Thank God now for this new life available in his Son,
       Jesus Christ. Thank him for one aspect of this salvation
       that you appreciate today.

=== DAY 5

13.   **Read Ephesians 4:25–32.**
       Paul outlines specific actions we are to take as Chris-
       tians. List these with verse numbers.
       (Example: v. 25—put off falsehood and speak truth
       with neighbor)

14.   Use the list above to identify an area in your life need-
       ing change or strengthening. Write it here.

15.   Describe one action you can take this week which will
       help you in this area. Pray that God's Holy Spirit will
       empower you to see this area of your life changed or
       strengthened beginning this very moment.

EPHESIANS 5

Once you lived in darkness, participating in dark thoughts and activities, but now you are light in Jesus Christ. Live as God's children, children of the light, in love and obedience to the Father.

If you are married, treat your spouse as God's loving relative, a member of the Church, the very body of Jesus Christ. Learn that it is possible to reflect in your relationships the mystery of Christ's love for you his Church, his Bride.

How can you make Christ's love and respect evident in your marriage today?

━━━━━━━━━━━━━━━━━━━━━━━━━━━━━━━ DAY 1

1. **Read Ephesians 5:1–7.**

   In the chart below list actions (with verse numbers) we are to pursue as Christians and those we are to resist.
   (Example: v. 1 - imitators of God live a life of love
           v. 3 - no hint of sexual immorality, impurity, greed)

Actions to be taken	Actions to be refused

Actions to be taken	Actions to be refused

2.   Look up these verses and discover who has the power
       to accomplish these things in our life if we rely upon
       him.
             Zechariah 4:6
             Luke 11:11–13
             John 14:26
             John 16:13–15
             Romans 8:9–14
             Romans 8:26–27
             Galatians 5:16–25

3.   Ask God to fill you to overflowing with his Holy Spirit
       in accord with Ephesians 5:18 so that you will be
       equipped to live the Christian life in his power.

== DAY 2

4.   **Read Ephesians 5:8–20.**
       In this passage Paul contrasts a life lived in "light" with
       life in "darkness," the "wise" with "foolish." List the
       characteristics of each.

Life in light/wise	Life in darkness/foolish
(Example: v. 8 - now light in the Lord, children of light)	(v. 8 - once darkness apart from God)

5.   Which of these characteristics would you like to experience more fully in your life?

6.   List ways you can begin now to live more completely as a wise child of Christ's light.

7.   **Read Ephesians 5:21–24.**
        List Paul's directives for wives.

8.   Define *submission* in your own words, identifying mis-
        conceptions others might have about this word.

9. (a) From verse 21 identify the goal and focus of biblical sub-
        mission and who is involved.

    (b) From these verses, what do you learn about God's love
        for you?
        Exodus 34:6

        Psalm 23:6

        Psalm 33:18

Psalm 100:5

Romans 8:35–39

1 John 3:1

(c) Ask God for a heart that loves him and desires to obey him in response to his overwhelming love toward you.

10.   **Read Ephesians 5:25–33.**
        List Paul's directives for husbands in these verses.

11.   What is Paul's final word for wives in verse 33?

12.   If your husband is not living according to these verses, you now have very specific ways to pray for him. Pray

about each item in your list under Question 10 and ask God to work these things into your husband's heart. Now ask God to give you a heart to respect your husband by appreciating those qualities in his life which first attracted you to him. List these below and thank God for the work he has done and is doing in your husband's life.

═══ **Day 5**

13.   **Reread Ephesians 5:21–33.**
       What do you learn about Jesus Christ in these verses?

14.   Christ constantly cares for us, his people. What should be our response to Christ?

Deuteronomy 6:5

Deuteronomy 10:12

Psalm 92:1–3

2 John 6

15.   Ask God to help you know him better, that your love for him might increase.

Ephesians 6

Children, parents, employees, employers—how do your relationships reflect Jesus' character and person? It is possible to do this only as you find your strength in Christ. This strength is supernaturally acquired.

It is a strength like armor that enables you to live God's way when the entire world pulls in an opposite direction. What are the elements of your armor? God's mighty power equips you with his truth, righteousness, faith, salvation, the Spirit, and God's Word.

Pray with the Spirit's power and you will stand firm and immovable. What is your stance today?

—————————————————————————————————— DAY 1

1.   **Read Ephesians 6:1–4.**
       According to these verses, how are children supposed to treat their parents?

2.   Are you lovingly instructing your children to be obedient and respectful while maintaining a reconciled relationship with them? List three ways to teach children to be respectful and obedient.

3.   Though no longer a child, do you pursue and maintain
        a reconciled relationship with your parents? Ask God
        this week to help you do whatever is necessary to
        accomplish reconciliation in your relationships with
        your parents and children. Pray that in all things, both
        your parents and your children will see the light and
        love of Jesus in your life.

━━━━━━━━━━━━━━━━━━━━━━━━━━━━━━━━━━━━━━ Day 2

4.   **Read Ephesians 6:5–9.**
        These verses can be applied to employer/employee
        relationships as well. List Paul's instructions to both:
        Employee

Employer

5. (a) How does Paul describe himself in Romans 1:1 and Philippians 1:1?

   (b) What do you think it means to be a "servant" of Christ?

6. (a) From this passage, what do you learn about being a "servant" of Christ?

   (b) Ask God to show you three ways you can live as Christ's servant this week and pray for the Holy Spirit's power to do so.

7.   **Read Ephesians 6:10–18.**
      What is the purpose of the armor of God?

8.   List the different parts of God's armor and describe each
      one.
      (Example: belt of truth = always speaking and acting in
      a truthful way.)

9.   (a) Explain your understanding of the phrase, "be strong
          in the Lord."

(b) Ask God to enable you to "be strong" in "his mighty power."

—————————————————————————— Day 4

10.   **Read Ephesians 6:19–20.**
        In these verses, what is Paul's request for prayer?

11.   From these verses, what can we learn about this aspect
        of our Christian life?
        Acts 4:29

        Philippians 1:14

        1 Peter 3:15–16

12.   Are you desiring each day to be a bold witness for Jesus
        Christ? Ask the Lord to help you overcome the fear of
        others' opinions, self-interest, shyness or any other atti-
        tude that keeps you from loving others enough to tell
        them about Jesus Christ, their only hope.

13.   **Read Ephesians 6:21–24.**
       What was Paul's purpose in sending Tychicus?

14.   Are you an "encourager"? List phrases from the verses
       below that describe our ministry of encouragement as
       members of Christ's body.
       Romans 12:8

       Romans 15:4, 5

       1 Thessalonians 4:18

       2 Timothy 4:2

       Hebrews 3:13

       Hebrews 10:25

15.   Pray now that God will enable you to be an encourager
        to those you meet each day this week. Pray, as Paul did
        in verse 23, that peace, love from faith in God, and his
        grace will touch the lives of those you love and strangers
        you meet each day.

PHILIPPIANS 1

While in chains for Christ, Paul prayed for the believers in Philippi whom he loved and considered partners in his ministry. His chains encouraged believers to courageously and fearlessly tell others about God's good news, the gospel. Spreading the gospel of Jesus Christ was Paul's highest call. His desire was that whether by his life or death, Jesus Christ would be exalted.

Learn about Paul's calling in this chapter. What is your highest calling?

DAY 1

1.   **Read Philippians 1:1–6.**
     Paraphrase Paul's greeting using your own words to describe the italicized words: Paul and Timothy, *servants of Christ Jesus* _____,
     to all the *saints in Christ Jesus* _____
     at Philippi, together with the *overseers and deacons* _____: *Grace* _____ and *peace* _____
     to you from God our Father and the Lord Jesus Christ.

2.   Use these verses to help you discover what "good work" Paul is referring to in verse 6.
     Psalm 138:8

1 Corinthians 1:8

Ephesians 2:10

From these verses identify who will accomplish this "good work" and why can he be trusted.

3.   List several Christian sisters or brothers whom you consider your partners in the Lord Jesus Christ (not including spouse or children). List ways you can pray for them about both their personal spiritual growth and ability to tell others about their faith in Christ.

Prayer partners in Christ	Specific prayer requests

Maybe you have never asked anyone to be a "partner" in prayer with you. Ask someone today. Begin the wonderful experience of true partnership in prayer encouraging one another as you grow in Christ Jesus.

―――――――――――――――――――――――――――――――― Day 2

4.   **Read Philippians 1:7–11.**

Write phrases from verses 7 and 8 which describe Paul's love and feelings of association with those he considers prayer partners.

5.   List Paul's specific prayer requests in verses 9–11.

6.   Pray the same phrases for your prayer partners today as you desire God's best for his glory, honor, and praise in your life.

——————————————————————————————— DAY 3

7.   **Read Philippians 1:12–18.**
       List benefits Paul sees as a result of his imprisonment.

8.   What is the highest goal in ministry for which Paul
        rejoices? If you are able, list other Scripture passages in
        the Bible where Paul sees the difficult experiences in his
        life as opportunities to make Jesus Christ known.

9.   List ways that the difficult situation in your life today
        can be used for God's glory. In both action and word,
        how can you use this situation to show others about
        your faith in Christ?

        Pray now that God will use your present circumstances to
enable you to grow in Christ and share your faith with others.

DAY 4

10.   **Read Philippians 1:18b–26.**
        Describe Paul's dilemma in this passage.

11.   How would you explain Paul's meaning in the phrase,
        "For to me, to live is Christ and to die is gain"?

12. (a) How does verse 21 apply to your life?

    (b) Have you committed your life to Jesus Christ in a way
        that he is the most important person in your life? Pray
        now and ask the Lord Jesus to remove any hindrance
        that causes you to hesitate. Give yourself totally to him
        today. It is a decision you will never regret. Read these
        verses for further insight.
        Romans 12:1–2

        Hebrews 12:1–3

———————————————————————— Day 5

13.   **Read Philippians 1:27–30.**
       In this passage, what was Paul's challenge to the Philip-
       pian believers?

14.   Study the following verses to discover Paul's meaning
       in Philippians 1:29.
       Matthew 5:11–12

       John 15:20–25

       Acts 5:41–42

15.   Read the following verses. Write a phrase for each
        describing the good that can grow out of difficult times.
        Ask God to accomplish his "good" in you and through
        you, using every circumstance in your life to "conform
        you to the image of his Son" (Romans 8:28–29) for his
        glory.
        2 Corinthians 12:9–10

        James 1:2–4

        1 Peter 1:3–9

PHILIPPIANS 2

Jesus Christ is and was God in the flesh. To know the character of God, look at Jesus. In this chapter Paul describes the attitude of Jesus which can infuse our lives.

Discover how his power makes his reflection in your life a daily possibility. Do your attitudes, actions, and motivations reflect Jesus Christ in you?

=== DAY 1

1. **Read Philippians 2:1–2**

   List the qualities found in the first two verses that Paul hopes characterize the Philippian believers.

2. How can the Philippian believers complete Paul's joy?

3. Give one example of how you could help fulfill each of these desires (v. 2) in your local church.

Ask the Holy Spirit to identify any area where you have fallen short and ask him to give you new insight and ideas for accomplishing these three directives.

―――――――――――――――――――――――――― DAY 2

4.   **Read Philippians 2:3–11.**
        Define (a) and (b) in your own words and describe ways you can "consider others better than yourselves."
    (a) selfish ambition

    (b) vain conceit

5.   How does Jesus Christ exemplify the attitude we are to
        have toward one another?

6.   Prayerfully ask the Father God to show you in the next
        week three ways you can be aware of the interests of
        others. List them here and ask him to make this a real-
        ity in your life this week.

———————————————————————————————————— Day 3

7.   **Read Philippians 2:12–18.**
        Using these verses, define the phrase "continue to work
        out your salvation with fear and trembling."

1 Corinthians 9:24–27

Hebrews 6:12

2 Peter 1:3–9

8.   How are you enabled to "work out your salvation" as defined above?

9.   Prayerfully ask God to fill you with his Holy Spirit, empowering you to experience the fullness of his salvation given to you now and forever.

10.   **Read Philippians 2:19–24.**
       Paul commended Timothy for expressing a certain quality. What was it?

11.   Make a comparison chart contrasting human personal interests with the interest of Jesus Christ.

       List as many pertinent Scripture references as you can.

Personal Interests	Christ's Interests
Example: Preoccupation with meals/food	John 6:27

12.   List three ways you can look out for the interests of Jesus Christ this week. Pray that the Lord will give you a heart to know and pursue his interests.

13.   **Read Philippians 2:25–30.**
        Paul writes "honor men like him." List the names of
        men and women like Epaphroditus in your life.
        How can you welcome and honor them?

14.   Write a note of appreciation today to your pastor, a sin-
        gle missionary, missionary family, or someone you feel
        has given his or her life for the work of Christ, extend-
        ing your hand of love to others you may never meet.
        Pray for that person each day this week asking God to
        equip him or her by the power of his Spirit for the work
        of ministry.

PHILIPPIANS 3

Paul considered everything worthless—a loss—compared to knowing Jesus Christ. Rather than looking back and focusing on past defeats or pleasures, Paul always looked forward, pressing on toward the final prize of eternity spent with God.

Examine your goal and focus. How can you, like Paul, press forward?

DAY 1

1.   **Read Philippians 3:1–6.**

In this chapter Paul speaks of the "Circumcision Party," those who demanded that Gentiles go through Jewish rites to be saved.

(a) What are Paul's instructions about this practice?

(b) Where do those who believed this doctrine place their confidence?

2.   If Paul were to place his confidence in the same rules
       as those who demanded circumcision, what were his
       credentials?

3.   Do you have human credentials that you are relying on
       for your relationship with God (number of years in
       church attendance, religious pursuits, Bible studies
       attended)? According to the following verses, what
       should give you confidence concerning your continued
       relationship with the Lord?
       John 1:12, 13

       John 15:5

       Romans 8:1–5

       2 Corinthians 3:4–6

Galatians 6:8

4.   **Read Philippians 3:7–9.**
      What does Paul identify as the all-encompassing pursuit of his life?

5.   List those things which you consider "a loss" compared to knowing Christ Jesus. How have your priorities, interests, and the things you value changed since you have come to know Jesus Christ?

6.   Identify anything in your life today that you feel is keeping you from this complete pursuit of knowing God. Pray now and ask the Lord to remove any love for the things of this world that would crowd out your love for him and desire to know him. Pray that Romans 12:1–2 will be accomplished in you.

7.   **Read Philippians 3:10–11.**
        Define each of the following phrases in your own words.
    (a) want to know Christ

    (b) the power of his resurrection

    (c) fellowship of sharing in his sufferings

    (d) becoming like him in his death

    (e) attain to the resurrection from the dead

8.   Positionally these things are ours in Christ already when
        we place our faith in him, but Paul was speaking expe-
        rientially. Paul desired to experience to the fullest all
        that the Lord Jesus Christ held for his life. Is that your
        desire today?

Write a prayer here and express to the Father the deepest desires of your heart as you read again meditatively Philippians 3:7–11.

———————————————————————— DAY 4

9.   **Read Philippians 3:12–16.**
      According to this passage, define the view we should take as we mature in Christ.

10.   Using verse 15, stop now and pray, asking God to show you if at any point you think differently. Ask him to correct your thinking.

11. (a) Explain Paul's meaning in verse 16.

(b) List ways you can fulfill this directive in your personal life this week. Ask the Father to make this possible as you seek to be empowered by the Holy Spirit to accomplish his will.

———————————————————————————— Day 5

12.   **Read Philippians 3:17–21.**
       How does Paul describe those who live as enemies of the cross of Christ?

13.   According to this passage, what is the Lord's promise to us as his followers?

14. (a) What does it mean to "eagerly await"?

(b) List ways that today you can exemplify this attitude of anticipation.

(c) According to this entire chapter, what can you do to make the wait more profitable?

Ask the Lord Jesus Christ to give you a more completely committed heart that you may grow more intimately acquainted with him each day, experiencing and enjoying the fellowship of his presence.

PHILIPPIANS 4

Is an anxiety-free life possible? Learn that with Christ all things are possible, so a life free from worry is available for the asking. God's peace beyond human understanding is yours by request.

Have you asked for this peace today?

═══ DAY 1

1. **Read Philippians 4:1–3.**
    Review Philippians chapter 3 and explain how we are to "stand firm in the Lord."

2. There is apparently some disagreement between Euodia and Syntyche. How does God view contention? According to the following verses, how are we instructed to resolve disagreement?
    Matthew 5:23–24

77

Matthew 18:15–19

Romans 12:16

Romans 15:5–6

Philippians 2:2–4

3.   Are you unreconciled with anyone today? Pray that
        God will give you the opportunity to go to this person,
        pursuing and securing reconciliation for his name's
        sake. From the following verses explain why reconcili-
        ation is so important to God.
        2 Corinthians 5:18–21

Colossians 1:21–23

─── DAY 2

4.   **Read Philippians 4:4–7.**
        (a) Define *rejoice* as found in the dictionary.

(b) Read John 16:17–28 and John 17:13 and define the true source of joy.

5. (a) List Paul's directives in Philippians 4:4–7.

(b) Why are we to do these things and what is the end result?

6. Are you living according to this passage today or are anxiety and worry eating away at the very fiber of your life and joy?

7.   **Read Philippians 4:8–9.**
      The way we use our mind can have a powerful effect
      on the way we live our lives. List each subject given in
      these two verses for acceptable thought patterns and
      habits.

8.   List three practical ways you can implement the direc-
      tions given in these two verses.

9.   Pray that God will fulfill his promise in the following
      verses as you seek to obey his directives by the Holy
      Spirit's power.
      Romans 12:2

      2 Corinthians 3:18

10.   **Read Philippians 4:10–13.**

According to this passage, what did Paul learn and what was the secret he discovered?

11.   According to these verses, what do you learn about contentment?
        Luke 3:12–14

        1 Timothy 6:6–12

        Hebrews 13:5

12.   Have you learned the secret of contentment as Paul did?

━━━━━━━━━━━━━━━━━━━━━━━━━━━━━━━━━━━ DAY 5

13.   **Read Philippians 4:14–23.**
        What does Paul identify as two results of cheerfully giving for the cause of Christ?

14.   What do you learn about the "sacrifice" Paul refers to
        from the following verses?
        Romans 12:1

        Ephesians 5:2

        Hebrews 13:15–16

15.   Paraphrase Philippians 4:23 in your own words defin-
        ing key words. Pray now that the Lord Jesus will make
        this real in your life throughout the coming week, giv-
        ing you peace and comfort.

COLOSSIANS 1

Faith in Christ Jesus, hope that is stored up for us in heaven, and love that springs from this hope are the qualities Paul identified for the Colossians. These are the fruit, the response, of lives touched by the gospel of God's grace.

This fruit testifies to God's rescue in each of our lives from the "dominion of darkness . . . into the kingdom of the Son he loves" (Colossians 1:13).

Christ is the very image of God. Paul describes Jesus' image and activity in securing our relationship with God. Learn in this chapter that the mystery of Christ in you, which is the hope of glory, is revealed to all who walk as Jesus walked.

Today are you walking as Christ walked?

━━━━━━━━━━━━━━━━━━━━━━━━━━━ DAY 1

1. **Read Colossians 1:1–8.**
   (a) From verses 1–4, identify the four qualities Paul sees in the Colossian Christians.

(b) Do you believe you exemplify these qualities? Why or why not?

2.   List specific facts you learn about the gospel in Colossians 1:1–7. Then define *gospel*.

3. (a) How are the qualities seen in the Colossian Christians directly related to the gospel?

    (b) Are you allowing the gospel of Jesus Christ to accomplish its full work in your life?

(c) Name three things you can do this week to allow the gospel to have a greater impact on your life.

―――――――――――――――――――――― Day 2

4.   **Read Colossians 1:9–14.**

(a) In verse 9, what did Paul and his companions specifically pray for the Colossians?

(b) What can you learn from the passages below about the different aspects of this prayer?
1 Thessalonians 4:3–8

1 Thessalonians 5:16–18

Hebrews 13:20–21

5.   According to verses 10–14, what was the reason for this
        prayer and Paul's desires for the Colossians?

6.   Take time to pause and meditate on these verses. Which
        specific aspect of Paul's prayer would you like to pray
        for yourself today? Ask God to accomplish this in your
        life beginning now.

DAY 3

7.   **Read Colossians 1:15–20.**
        List with verses, the qualities identified with Christ.

8.   What more do you learn about Christ in the following
        verses?
        John 1:18

        John 3:16, 18

        1 John 4:9–10

9.   Give thanksgiving to God now for the greatness of the
        Lord Jesus Christ, who would humble himself to live
        among us and die on the cross for our sin.

─── Day 4

10.   **Read Colossians 1:21–23.**
        Using this passage, describe the change in a person's
        position before God and relationship to God when
        he/she believes on the Lord Jesus Christ.

11.   Explain if, when, and how this change has occurred in your life. Come prepared to share this if it is your desire to do so.

━━━━━━━━━━━━━━━━━━━━━━━━━━━━━━━━ DAY 5

12.   **Read Colossians 1:24–29.**

   (a) In this passage, Paul rejoices in suffering. What value does he see in his suffering?

   (b) What insight do you gain from the following verses concerning this suffering?

   Acts 5:41–42

   2 Corinthians 6:3–10

Philippians 1:27–29

1 Peter 4:12–19

1 Peter 5:8–9

13. (a) Describe Paul's ministry as he sees it in verses 25–29.

    (b) Whose power makes it possible for Paul to fulfill his commission for ministry?

14. (a) Read 2 Corinthians 4:7–12. Pray now to be a vessel empty of selfish ambition and concern. Pray to be filled to overflowing with Christ's Spirit, to be used by him to share his good news.
    (b) List the names of those whose lives you are affecting today for Jesus Christ.

COLOSSIANS 2

Through faith in Christ and his death, the payment of sin's penalty is made. Our sins are forgiven and the written code of God's judgment that was against us and opposed us is cancelled, nailed to the cross.

Faith produces unspeakable freedom. Freedom is restrained only to the degree that love for God stimulates and restrains us. Learn that all we do can be an expression of our overwhelming gratitude to God.

Do your actions reflect joyful freedom and loving gratitude?

_____ DAY 1

1.   **Read Colossians 2:1–5.**

   (a) What was the purpose in Paul's struggles?

   (b) Where is true wisdom and knowledge found?

2.   Read the following verses and note phrases that give
        further insight into these qualities.
        Psalm 111:10
        Psalm 119:66
        Proverbs 2:1–5

        Proverbs 8:10–11

        Romans 11:33–36

        Ephesians 4:10–13

3.   How can you grow in the knowledge and wisdom of
        God?

     Pray and ask God to replace your human knowledge and
rationalizations with his knowledge and his wisdom. Your family and friends may be looking to you for insight and direction.
Be sure they receive godly insight and wisdom based on God's
word and knowledge of his person.

── DAY 2

4.   **Read Colossians 2:6–8.**
        (a) What is Paul's challenge to each of us in verses 6–7?

(b) List three practical ways you can do this.

5.   Identify three examples of "hollow and deceptive phi-
        losophy" (dependent on human tradition and the basic
        principles of this world rather than Christ) found in our
        culture or churches.

6.   Name several resources God has given you today to
        enable you to walk firmly with Christ, protecting you
        from empty philosophies and deceitful or worthless
        pursuits. Pause and thank the Lord for his continued
        love and protection as he draws you nearer to himself
        each day.

7. **Read Colossians 2:9–15.**

   List with verses every fact you learn about Jesus Christ from this passage.

8. God accomplished great and mighty things for you through his Son, Jesus. Reread this passage inserting your name for the word *you*.

9. Write a prayer thanking God today for performing all these actions, which he alone could perform, because of his great love for you.

10.   **Read Colossians 2:16–19.**

In this passage, what is Paul warning us about ?

11.   According to these verses, what has happened to those who have adopted pseudo-spiritual speculations and practices?

12.   It has been said that to identify the counterfeit, one must be fully familiar with the true. How does this apply to your Christian life as you seek to remain faithful and steady in your walk with Christ this week?

━━━━━━━━━━━━━━━━━━━━━━━━━━━━━ DAY 5

13.   **Read Colossians 2:20–23.**

Identify rules in our churches today that are based on human commands and teachings.

14. (a) What appearance do these rules give?

   (b) What do these rules lack?

15.   Define *sensual indulgence* and explain why outside prac-
       tices do not bring change in these areas. Are there strug-
       gles in your life today which you are seeking to allevi-
       ate through external activity?

   Pray now and ask the Holy Spirit to identify these areas for
you. Begin to trust Jesus Christ's power living in you (as
described in Romans 8:11) to transform your life within, free-
ing you from the captivity of destructive habits and practices.
Let Jesus Christ reproduce his victory in you by his mighty
power.

COLOSSIANS 3

"And whatever you do, whether in word or deed, do it all in the name of the Lord Jesus, giving thanks to God the Father through him" (Colossians 3:17). Wives, husbands, children, parents, employees, what motivates your attitudes and actions? Explore the possibility that all you do can be done in joyful recognition of God's love and in service to his Son.

What motivates you today?

DAY 1

1.   **Read Colossians 3:1–4.**
     In this passage, what are we instructed to do?

2.   Define the following phrases:
     you have been raised with Christ

     set your heart on things above

96

set your minds on things above

your life is now hidden with Christ in God

Christ, who is your life

3.   List three practical actions you can take this week to
       ensure your obedience to these verses.
       1.

       2.

       3.

   Thank your heavenly Father now for the position in and with
Christ you hold as his privileged and precious child.

─── Day 2

4.   **Read Colossians 3:5–11.**
   (a) List all the practices in this passage which we are to "put
       to death" as Christians.

   (b) Explain how you can do this.

5. (a) Explain your understanding of verses 9 and 10.

   (b) Write phrases from the following verses for further insight.
       Romans 6:6–14

       Romans 13:14

       2 Corinthians 5:17

       Ephesians 4:22–24

6.   **Read Colossians 3:12–17.**

        List the instructions we are given for life "as God's cho-
        sen people, holy and dearly loved."

7.   What is to be our attitude as we desire to live this life
        pleasing to God?

8.   List three practical things you can do this week to ful-
        fill the directives in this passage. Pray for the Holy
        Spirit's power to be actively at work in your life, accom-
        plishing God's purposes for his glory.

9.   **Read Colossians 3:18–21.**

These verses give direction for each of us as we func-
tion within our family. List and explain each directive.

10. (a) For whom are we to fulfill each directive?

    (b) How does this affect your attitude in fulfilling each
        instruction?

11.   Ask the Father to show you this week three ways you
        can submit to your husband—ways that are specifically
        "fitting in the Lord." If you are single, list three ways
        you can honor a family member in a manner that
        "pleases the Lord."

12.   Ask God now to forgive you for any hostile, resentful,
        angry, or resistant feelings you have toward a family
        member or God himself (whether or not you feel justi-
        fied in these feelings, according to Psalm 51:1–4, they
        only hurt you and God). Pray for the healing love of Jesus
        and his Word, liberating you to realize that only in rec-
        onciliation and obedience to God's word is there true
        and lasting peace, joy, and freedom from sin's captivity.

13.   **Read Colossians 3:22–25.**
       What attitudes are we to exemplify in all work that we
       do for employers or leaders in authority over us?

14.   How does this apply to all the service we perform
       within the church body?

15.   Ask the Lord Jesus to show you specific ways you can
       exemplify the attitudes listed in these four verses,
       whether at work, at home, or in your church responsi-
       bilities. There is no greater privilege than being used by
       the Lord Jesus to live out his truth with others for the
       advancement of his kingdom on earth.

COLOSSIANS 4

Final words of persevering devotion close Paul's letter. Request for prayer and greetings from fellow servants of Christ are expressed.

Are you encouraged to walk close to Christ today? How can you encourage someone else to do the same?

DAY 1

1. **Read Colossians 4:1–4.**

   How are we to treat those who are under our authority, such as children in Sunday school, VBS, others in committees, etc.? Can you give personal examples of ways to show the Master's love and guidance in dealing with others?

2. From this passage, list Paul's directions for prayer.

3.   Examine your prayer life. For whom are you praying
        daily, and in what manner? Whose ministry are you
        upholding in prayer? List three ways you can enhance
        your prayer life this week or methods of prayer that
        have been especially helpful to you. Be prepared to
        share these.

————————————————————————————————————— DAY 2

4.   **Read Colossians 4:5–6.**
        Explain your understanding of these verses.

5. From the following passages, what can we learn about our verbal communication with others?
Proverbs 22:11

James 3:5–8

1 Peter 3:15–16

6. Pray now that Psalm 141:3 will be accomplished by the Lord in your life, empowering you to use your speech for his glory, honor, and praise.

────────────────────────────── DAY 3

7. **Read Colossians 4:7–9.**
What qualities does Paul identify and appreciate in Tychicus?

8.   What qualities do you identify and appreciate about the
        following people?
        Your pastor

        Your husband

        Each of your children

        A friend

        A co-worker

9.   Take the opportunity (based on Hebrews 10:24) to do
        as Paul did—commend someone for his or her exam-
        ple of Christ's character. Pray today that you might be
        more "conformed to the likeness of his Son" each day
        so that others will see Christ in you.

10.   **Read Colossians 4:10–18.**

In sending the final greetings of others, Paul highlights Epaphras's prayer. Write that prayer here and explain its meaning.

11.   List verses of Scripture that you have prayed in the past or would desire to pray in the future for others in your life.

12.   Praying Scripture (asking God for the promises in his Word to be fulfilled for you or another) is a powerful tool in accomplishing God's purposes.

   (a) Which verse of Scripture would you desire to see God fulfill in you this week?

(b) Describe an experience when God's word in prayer gave you hope, direction, or encouragement during a difficult time. Thank God for giving you his Word and providing you with guidance and sustenance for all of life.

—————————————————————————————— DAY 5

13.   Quietly and prayerfully think back over this whole study. Write out three verses (one from each book: Ephesians, Philippians and Colossians) that have been particularly meaningful to you. Be prepared to explain why these verses have affected your life during the last few months.

14.   List new insights concerning the Lord Jesus Christ himself you have received from this study. Include verses if possible.

15.   Write one specific prayer request for yourself incorporating the truths you have learned in Ephesians, Philippians, and Colossians. Ask God to accomplish his will in and through you as you seek to draw near to him each day.

Thank God now for his love that cherishes, preserves, and keeps you as you are in the process of becoming all he created you to be!

For more information concerning the formation and maintenance of vibrant, effective small and large group Bible studies using Linda McGinn's *Women in the Word* Bible study series, please contact:

Roz Soltau
Women in the Word
    Coordinator
(305) 782-7506

Donna Robb
Key Point Radio Network
P.O. Box 5598
Asheville, NC 28803
1-800-948-0745 or
(704) 686-0860

Notes

Notes

Notes